CONTENTS

KU-152-524

WORKING IN SPACE

Space is the most extreme and hostile environment to survive in. There is no air for humans to breathe and no supply of food or shelter. Yet Space has always fascinated people. For hundreds of years, astronomers have peered at the night sky through telescopes, observing and trying to make sense of the Universe.

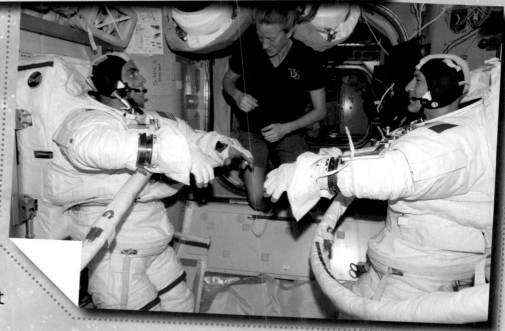

▲ Astronauts practise everything they do in Space in labs on Earth first, in order to anticipate and avoid possible problems.

Wide Open Space

Space begins 100 kilometres (62 miles) above the ground, where the atmosphere is too thin for aircraft to fly. To reach Space, a spacecraft has to travel fast enough to overcome the force of gravity. The first rockets powerful enough to do this were only developed about 60 years ago.

◀ Modern telescopes take incredible photos of stars and galaxies trillions of kilometres away. This photo shows a star dying.

This close up of Saturn and its rings was taken by an unmanned spacecraft called *Cassini*.

Humans in Space

Between 1968 and 1972, seven spacecraft and 24 astronauts made the 400,000-kilometre (nearly 250,000-mile) journey to the Moon. Since then, astronauts have been confined to orbiting Earth. At present, the only habitat for humans in Space is the International Space Station (ISS), which orbits about 354 kilometres (220 miles) above Earth.

Exploring Space

Scientists study Space to try to understand how the Universe began and how it works. They are searching for traces of life on other planets and for minerals that could be useful to humans on Earth. Scientists also use satellites in Space to study events on Earth, such as floods and forest fires, rising sea levels and air pollution. In this book we will look at how space scientists carry out their research, what they do with the results, and some of the discoveries they have made.

DANGER!

Lack of air to breathe is not the only hazard facing astronauts in Space. The temperature changes from extremely hot (100° Celsius) in sunlight to extremely cold (-100° Celsius) in shadow. In addition to this, lethal amounts of radiation from solar particles and cosmic rays can strike with little or no warning.

WHAT'S OUT THERE?

As telescopes become increasingly sensitive, astronomers are obtaining more and more information about the Universe. They have seen the birth and death of stars and extraordinary phenomena, including supernovas (massive exploding stars), white dwarfs and distant galaxies.

▼ An artist used information collected by a spacecraft to create this picture of a 13-billion-year-old black hole.

Vast Distances

The Universe is unimaginably huge. *Gaia*, a space observatory (see page 19), is plotting a billion stars, but they are just one per cent of the total stars in our galaxy, the Milky Way. The Milky Way is one galaxy out of hundreds of billions. The distances between galaxies are so vast they cannot be measured in kilometres or miles. Instead, they are measured in light-years. A light-year is the distance travelled by light in one year – nearly 10 trillion kilometres (about 6 trillion miles)!

Looking Back in Time

Because distances in Space are so immense, astronomers are looking back in time as well as over distance. For example, if they observe a supernova 13,000 light-years away, it took 13,000 years for the light of that supernova explosion to reach them. This means the explosion happened 13,000 years ago!

> The Whirlpool Galaxy is one of the brightest galaxies in the sky. Its stars form a spiral around the centre.

⬇ Telescopes that orbit Earth in Space take very clear and detailed photos. These two distant galaxies are called Arp 273.

DANGER!

Astronomers think there is a black hole at the centre of every galaxy. A black hole is not actually a hole: it forms when a megastar collapses into a tiny space. Its gravity is so immense that it pulls in stars, planets and everything around it. Nothing can escape, not even light. Scientists can detect a black hole from the cloud of gas that glows brighter and brighter as it spirals into the hole.

TREADING LIGHTLY

Exploring Space is not easy for researchers working on the edge. Every planet and moon is a unique and different world, and scientists want to explore each one to find out what is there. They send probes and robot rovers to take dust samples and analyze the atmosphere. However, at the same time, they have to be very careful that the probes and rovers do not contaminate or change the natural state of the places on which they land.

Looking for Life

Space scientists look for signs of life elsewhere in the solar system, but they need to be sure that anything they find has not been accidentally taken there from Earth. Every part of every rover and probe is cleaned, sterilized and checked to make sure that it carries no cells or DNA from life on Earth.

An astronaut on the ISS checks the toilet waste disposal system to make sure that no waste is leaking into Space.

Bringing Space to Earth

The astronauts who landed on the Moon brought back samples but none of the spacecraft that have landed on other planets or moons have returned to Earth. However, the next Mars robot will collect samples that one day may be returned to Earth. When that happens, scientists must make sure the samples contain no alien bacteria or viruses that might be dangerous to Earth.

Scientists wear protective suits to assemble *Curiosity* and get it ready for launch.

CUTTING EDGE

Curiosity, a robot rover, is exploring the surface of Mars. Its mission is to find out whether there might ever have been minute forms of life on Mars in the past. *Curiosity* is the largest rover to land anywhere beyond Earth. It has six wheels and a nuclear-powered engine. It drills samples of rock and sends back information about them to Earth.

Tracks left by *Curiosity*'s wheels during its first test drive on Mars.

SCIENCE ON THE MOVE

One of the greatest challenges scientists working on the edge face is how to travel around Space. The Moon is about 405,000 kilometres (252,000 miles) away, but that distance is small compared to the distances between Earth and the other planets. For example, Jupiter is about 800 million kilometres (500 million miles) from Earth. Saturn is twice as far away as Jupiter, and Saturn is only halfway to Uranus!

▼ This picture of *Juno* flying over Jupiter's north pole was created by an artist years before the spacecraft reached the planet.

Finding Out More

Scientists use unmanned spacecraft to find out about the planets. An unmanned spacecraft has several advantages over a manned one. It can be much smaller and it does not have to return to Earth. This makes it much cheaper than a manned craft. Unmanned spacecraft have flown past and photographed every planet in the solar system and some of their moons.

Ongoing Missions

Cassini is an unmanned spacecraft that reached Saturn in 2004 and will explore the planet and its moons until 2017. In 2005 it dropped a probe called *Huygens* onto Titan, Saturn's largest moon. *Juno*, an unmanned craft that the National Aeronautics and Space Administration (NASA) launched in 2011, is expected to finally reach Jupiter in 2016. It will fly closer to Jupiter than any previous craft. *Voyager 1* was launched in 1977 and by 2013 it was 18.5 billion kilometres (11.5 billion miles) from the Sun. It is the first spacecraft to leave the solar system and travel through interstellar Space.

Curiosity took this picture of itself, which allowed engineers at mission control to check the condition of the rover.

DANGER!

Every part of *Curiosity*, the Mars rover launched in 2011, was carefully cleaned. Before the launch, however, a box containing three drill bits was opened and one drill bit was fixed to the drill head. This broke the rules for avoiding contamination. Luckily, no harm was done, because *Curiosity* will not travel to a site that might have liquid water or water ice within reach of the drill bits.

SPACE LAB

The ISS orbits Earth at a height of about 400 kilometres (250 miles) above the ground, and so the only way to reach it is in a spacecraft launched by rocket. Astronauts from different countries live and work together on the Space Station. The Station provides living space and science laboratories in several interconnected modules.

Scientists working on the ISS examine and make external repairs to the Station while attached to a robotic arm.

Building the Space Station

The Station is owned and run by space agencies in the United States (NASA), Europe (the European Space Agency), Russia, Canada and Japan. The first module was launched by Russia in November 1998. The rest of the Station was built over the next 12 years. It now has two main sections attached to a central truss, with several solar panels which generate electricity for the Station.

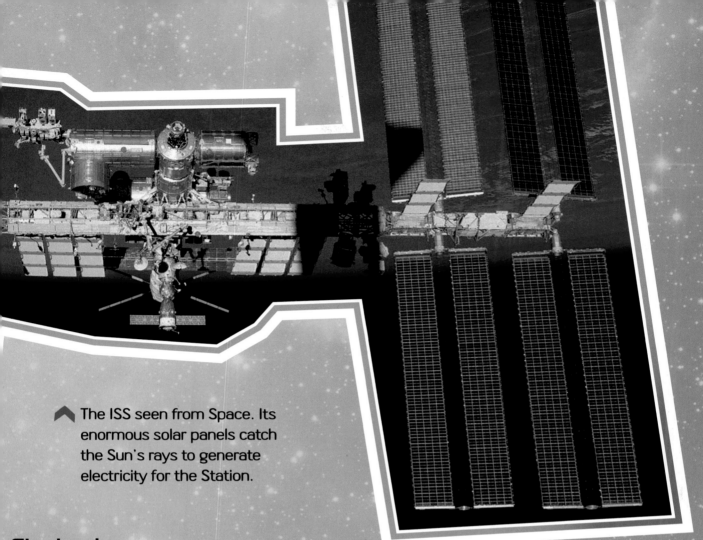

The ISS seen from Space. Its enormous solar panels catch the Sun's rays to generate electricity for the Station.

Air Lock

The Space Station has its own air, which is recycled and conditioned. It is vital that air does not escape or leak out. This means that entering and leaving the Station is done through a special entry lock. When a spacecraft, such as *Soyuz*, arrives at the Station, it is manoeuvred so that it makes a tight fit with the Station's docking port. The dock is then opened to allow access between the spacecraft and the Station.

DANGER!

The control module contains the Station's engines and is the control centre for the Space Station. In an emergency, all astronauts in the Station gather there to find out what has happened and to quickly deal with the situation. The greatest dangers are an air leak, a fire and the air turning poisonous.

SCIENCE IN SPACE

Astronauts on the ISS are the only scientists who work in Space. A crew of six astronauts works on the Station for several months at a time. These astronauts spend their working days maintaining the Station, installing new equipment and carrying out experiments.

Microgravity

The Space Station and everything on it is weightless. It feels as if the Space Station has escaped from Earth's gravity, but in fact it is in a state of freefall, or microgravity. Many experiments conducted there test the effect of microgravity on materials, plants and the astronauts' own bodies.

Supplying the Station

The Space Station is re-stocked every few months. An unmanned spacecraft called an Automated Transfer Vehicle (ATV) arrives from Earth with supplies of food and other items. Once the ATV has been unloaded, it is filled with rubbish and waste. Then it is jettisoned and, as it drops back to Earth, it burns up in the atmosphere, destroying the rubbish.

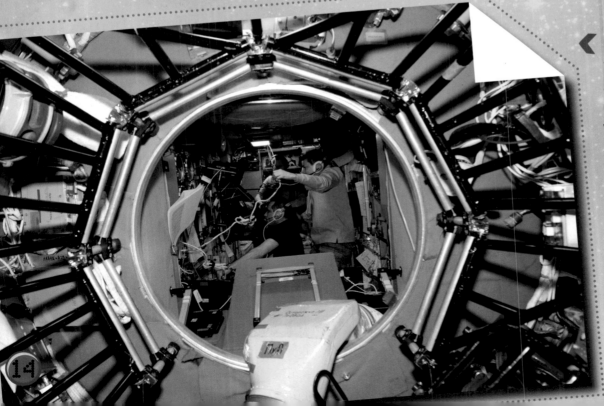

Scientists control the approach and safe docking of an unmanned supply vehicle to the Space Station.

Mission Control

Astronauts are constantly in touch with scientists back on Earth. Each space agency in the ISS has several mission control centres on the ground, which monitor their own components and activities. As the Space Station travels around Earth at nearly 30,000 kilometres per hour (18,600 miles per hour) it connects with different control centres on the ground.

For many years the space shuttle *Endeavour* brought NASA astronauts and components to the ISS.

The ISS has a manipulator arm which is controlled remotely. It is used to service and maintain the Station.

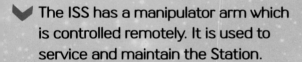

CUTTING EDGE

In 2013, astronauts on the ISS installed an amazing new technology that uses ultrasound to detect air leaks. Up until then, astronauts had to listen for the faint hissing sound of a leak and evacuate the spaceship if they could not locate it. The new technology means they can plug the tiniest leak before it causes any problems.

LIFE IN THE LAB

Living in microgravity affects everything the astronauts do. In Space there are no floors or ceilings and everything floats unless it is fixed down. The modules of the ISS are like corridors, no wider than an astronaut's outstretched arms. This makes it easier for astronauts to reach things and to move by pushing themselves off the sides. Food is prepared on Earth and then heated in a microwave oven. Liquids are contained in packages with straws.

Packages of food float freely in the service module of the ISS.

Sleeping in Space

The Station orbits Earth every 1.5 hours, so astronauts move between daylight and darkness every 45 minutes. To overcome this, the astronauts keep to a 24-hour timetable for waking and sleeping. When it is time to sleep, the astronaut slides into a sleeping bag. The sleeping bag may be attached to a wall or be in a sleeping station, which is like a large cupboard with drawers.

Without gravity or exercise, an astronaut's muscles become very weak so it is essential to exercise for several hours each day.

Space Walks

Sometimes an astronaut has to work on the outside of the Space Station, perhaps to adjust a solar panel or repair a component. An expedition outside the Station is called a space walk. Space walks are the most dangerous time for an astronaut and they may last several hours.

This astronaut has zipped himself into a sleeping bag to demonstrate how it is used.

DANGER!

A space suit is essential for a space walk. It provides the astronaut with oxygen to breathe and protects him or her from extreme temperatures and radiation. If the suit is torn, however, by a micrometeoroid or a tiny chip from the Space Station, it becomes useless. Astronauts also have to be extremely careful to stay attached to the Space Station. If they floated away, they would never be seen again.

BACK ON EARTH

Only a few lucky space scientists actually go into Space. Backing them up is a large team of scientists, engineers and support staff on the ground. Most space scientists and astronomers spend their lives on Earth, working in observatories, universities and space centres. Today, astronomers seldom even gaze into the night sky. Instead they work on information and images which are fed from Space into their computers.

▼ The spacecraft *Gaia* was transported from Europe in cargo planes and assembled in French Guiana.

Space Missions

Scientists plan missions and work out how the astronauts or spacecraft will achieve what they set out to do. If the mission is to the ISS, scientists are constantly in touch with the astronauts about the progress of the mission. Spacecraft and landers collect and send back huge amounts of data about the planets and moons they fly past or visit. Scientists may work on the data for years, analyzing and trying to understand it.

00:00:00:00

MCDONNELL DOUGLAS

Mission control at Cape Canaveral in Florida, USA, is one of many control centres around the world.

Astronomers

Astronomers study the stars. Some telescopes pick up radio waves from distant stars, while others collect light. The clearest views of Space come from telescopes that orbit Earth in Space. The *Hubble* telescope collects data and images from deep Space. *Keppler*, which was launched in 2009, can detect stars that have planets orbiting them.

CUTTING EDGE

In 2013 the European Space Agency launched *Gaia*, a space observatory with two space telescopes. Astronomers will use the telescopes to plot the positions of a 1,000 million stars to make a 3-D map of the Milky Way. It will use the two telescopes in the same way we use our eyes to measure how far away something is.

SEARCHING FOR LIFE

Is Earth the only planet in the Universe where life exists? The search for life is one of the most exciting and intriguing projects in which space scientists are involved. Although scientists have ruled out the possibility of finding intelligent alien life in the solar system, they are still looking for signs of simple life, such as bacteria. Further afield, scientists are looking for stars that have planets like Earth orbiting them, in case they can support life.

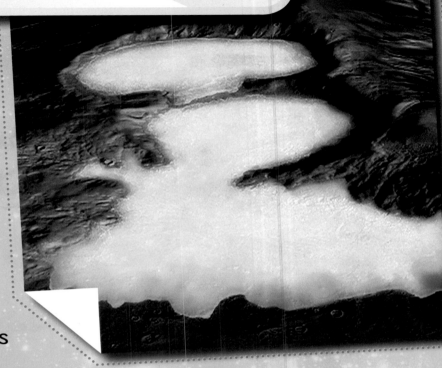

An artist's view of an ice sheet on Mars.

Signs of Life

All living things need water to survive, so scientists look for water or signs that water existed in the past. Mars, for example, has ice caps at its poles, like Earth, and *Curiosity* has found signs that water once flowed over its surface. By looking for fossils, scientists can see if life existed in the past.

Phoenix Mars Lander was one of *Curiosity*'s predecessors. Its instruments confirmed the presence of water ice on Mars.

Aliens Alert

If alien life exists elsewhere in our galaxy, how will scientists find it? First, they use the *Keppler* space telescope to identify stars that have planets orbiting them. Earth is sometimes called the 'Goldilocks planet', because it is neither too close to the Sun nor too far from it. Astronomers look for planets that are orbiting similar suns to ours, at distances that could be 'just right' for life.

This is an artist's view of one of the robots that could be orbiting Jupiter's icy moons in 2026, to assess whether life may exist below the moons' ice.

CUTTING EDGE

In August 2013, astronomers found their most Earth-like planet to date. It is 57 light-years away and its glowing pink image was seen through *Subaru*, an infrared telescope on Hawaii. It is four times as large as Jupiter and scientists estimate that its temperature is a sizzling 237° Celsius (460° Fahrenheit). Although the planet is similar to Earth, its temperature is too hot for life to survive there.

OUR SOLAR SYSTEM

Space scientists are not only looking for signs of life in the solar system. They also want to know what each planet consists of, how the solar system formed and what is happening now. There could be supplies of minerals out there that are already running low on Earth, although mining and transporting them to Earth is not yet possible. In recent years scientists have been most interested in Mars, Jupiter, Saturn and the asteroids.

Life on Mars

NASA plans to launch the next rover to Mars in 2020. Its mission will be to look for signs of past life and to collect samples. The samples collected will be stored in a cache, so that a future mission may be able to bring them back to Earth.

Saturn's Moon

When the *Huygens* probe landed on Titan in 2005 (see page 11), it sent back

pictures of a landscape that looks like Earth but is actually very different. Clouds and rivers are formed of liquid methane not water, and the 'rocks' are ice. Nevertheless, scientists are excited because they think that conditions on Titan may help them to understand how life began on Earth.

◀ Titan, one of Saturn's moons, is surrounded by a thick atmosphere and methane clouds.

Mining Asteroids

Asteroids are chunks of rock that orbit the Sun in the vast space between Mars and Jupiter. Scientists have landed unmanned spacecraft on two of the larger asteroids. Mining companies are interested in mining asteroids for precious metals.

Asteroids vary in size from large rocks to the dwarf planet Ceres, which is 1,000 kilometres (600 miles) across.

Jupiter's Great Red Spot is a massive storm that has been blowing for at least 400 years. The Spot is three times as large as the diameter of Earth.

DANGER!

Asteroids often wander from their orbit and crash into planets, including Earth. Scientists have identified several asteroids that could be dangerous to Earth and are tracking them. They are working out how to divert any asteroid that threatens Earth.

BILLION-DOLLAR SPACE

Space research can be expensive. It is thought that the cost for the Russian spacecraft *Soyuz* to take three astronauts to and from the ISS is about US$50 million. The United States is developing *Orion*, a new spacecraft and launch system to carry six astronauts to the ISS and beyond. The project is expected to cost about US$210 billion over 20 years.

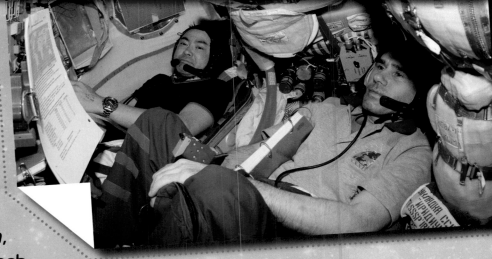

Two astronauts train for their return to Earth from ISS in a *Soyuz* spacecraft.

Paying for Research

In the 1960s the United States and the Soviet Union spent huge sums of money as they competed to land the first humans on the Moon. The United States spent about US$20.5 billion, which was equivalent to about US$100 billion in 2010. All of this money came from the US government, and governments continue to fund research. Now, however, countries cooperate with each other and in that way share the costs.

This equipment is mounted on the outside of the ISS and provides a low-cost and quick way of testing how particular materials behave in Space.

Spreading the Cost

The ISS is expected to cost 100 billion euros, but that cost is shared between several countries and spread over many years. Europe's share, for example, is about 8 billion euros over nearly 30 years. Some countries have schemes to raise extra money. Russia, for example, sells places on *Soyuz* for US$35 million each.

▼ Time and money is spent designing and testing equipment to make sure it is suitable for Space.

CUTTING EDGE

Orion will travel nearly 6,000 kilometres (3,600 miles) away from Earth and back again. The vehicle is called a multi-purpose crew vehicle (MPCV) and will be used to take astronauts and supplies to and from the ISS and possibly even to Mars.

RICHES OF SPACE

Who benefits from space research? The answer is that we all do. In the last 50 to 60 years, hundreds of satellites have been launched into Space to orbit Earth. They have changed the way we do things, including communications, weather forecasting and navigation. Many experiments carried out in Space have led to the development of medicines and technology on Earth.

⌄ This astronaut is testing how well his eyes and brain work together without gravity to judge height.

High-Tech Wonders

Many things that we use include technology developed in or for Space, although we may not realize it. Experiments in Space have led to infrared thermometers, insoles for sports shoes that protect the feet by absorbing shock, extra-nourishing baby food and many other things. Thanks to space research, firefighters now have breathing apparatus with supplies of air that last longer than in the past.

Connecting and Monitoring

Satellites in Space gather information about what is happening on Earth. They measure changes in the atmosphere, the oceans, coral reefs and glaciers as a result of climate change. Satellites are used in disaster relief and to map forest fires. Communications satellites transmit radio, television and mobile telephone signals. In fact modern society would quickly grind to a halt without satellites. Mobile phone networks, air traffic control, ships, police and emergency vehicles all rely on satellites for the Global Positioning System (GPS).

The ISS has many special devices and compartments for carrying out experiments. This scientist is working in the Microgravity Science Glovebox.

CUTTING EDGE

People who suffer from asthma could soon benefit from a small gadget developed in Space. Asthma is caused by inflammation in the narrow airways inside the lungs. The gadget detects when the user's airways are becoming inflamed so that the condition can be treated before the person is even aware of it.

This space experiment is studying how the lack of gravity affects the way that plants grow.

INTO THE FUTURE

Space is limitless, but space research is limited by the amount of money governments are willing to spend on it. Many ideas and projects for future space research are already being developed and planned. One of the most advanced is a mission to explore Jupiter and its icy planets. A more recent idea is to capture an asteroid and bring it closer to Earth, but the most ambitious project of all is to put astronauts on Mars.

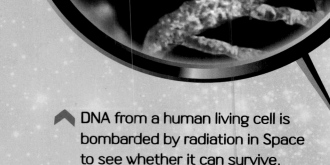

▼ This spacecraft is giving scientists a better understanding of how the Sun affects Earth's upper atmosphere.

▲ DNA from a human living cell is bombarded by radiation in Space to see whether it can survive.

2020 and Beyond

The European Space Agency plans to launch JUICE (Jupiter Icy moons Explorer) in 2022. It will orbit Jupiter, before flying past the moons Callisto, Europa and Ganymede, which may have alien life in oceans below their icy surfaces. NASA is working out how an unmanned spacecraft could capture an asteroid and drag it into orbit around the Moon, where robots or astronauts could reach it.

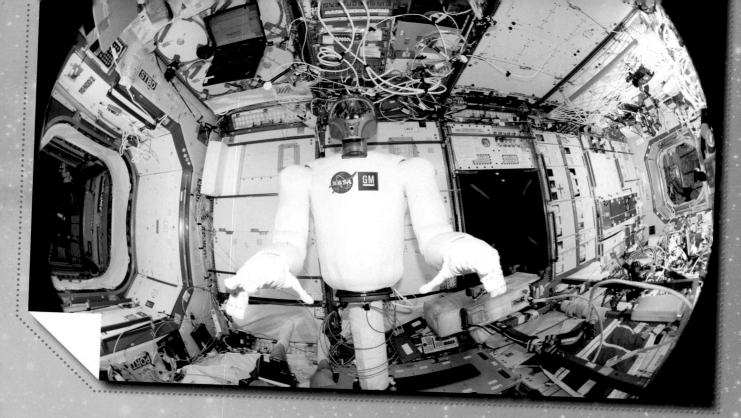

R2 is a space robot which may take over some of the most dangerous tasks on the ISS, such as monitoring air flow.

Astronauts on Mars?

The 56-million-kilometre (35-million-mile) journey from Earth to Mars would take about 10 months. Before astronauts can even set off, however, unmanned spacecraft and robots would have to prepare a special habitat on Mars, stocked with supplies of food, fuel and other essentials, for them to live. Scientists are hoping to use water below the ice to manufacture fuel for a rocket to launch them on their return journey.

DANGER!

Mars is no holiday destination. The atmosphere is very thin and consists mostly of carbon dioxide. The average temperature at the equator is -30° Celsius, as cold as Antarctica. Astronauts would need to put on space suits before they ventured outside their habitat. Despite these difficulties, astronauts are already being recruited and trained for a mission to Mars!

GLOSSARY

asteroids Small rocky objects that orbit the Sun.

astronomer A scientist who studies the stars, planets, moons and everything else in Space.

atmosphere A mixture of gases that surround a planet or moon.

black hole A region of Space where gravity is so strong that even light cannot escape or reflect back from it.

cache A secure store.

DNA An acronym for deoxyribonucleic acid. DNA is located in the nuclei of cells, which make up the body.

docking port A special place on a spacecraft or space station where spacecraft can form an airtight connection.

galaxies Vast groups of stars that travel together through Space. Our solar system is in the Milky Way galaxy.

Global Positioning System (GPS) A way of pinpointing a position on Earth by using signals from satellites in Space.

habitat A place to live.

infrared telescope A telescope that picks up invisible waves just beyond the red end of the colour spectrum.

infrared thermometer A thermometer that can measure body temperature from a person's ear canal.

lander Part of a spacecraft that lands on a planet or moon.

microgravity The condition of being weightless in Space.

micrometeoroid A very small meteoroid, such as a speck of space dust or a tiny chip of rock from an asteroid.

mission control centre A control centre on Earth that manages missions in Space.

modules Standard sections that form part of a whole.

orbiting Travelling in a set path around another body, such as the Sun or a planet.

probe Part of a spacecraft containing instruments for analyzing materials.

radiation Energy that travels from a source across Space.

robot rover A vehicle controlled by a computer.

satellite An object that has been launched into orbit around Earth for a particular purpose, such as transmitting communications signals or photographing the surface of Earth.

solar particles High-energy particles emitted by the Sun.

sterilized Treated to kill all living things, such as bacteria and viruses.

supernovas Explosions of massive stars.

truss A strong structure that supports other structures.

ultrasound A sound wave that is too high pitched for humans to hear.

unmanned Without a crew.

white dwarf A star that is no longer burning and has collapsed into a dense but small object.

FURTHER READING

Books

100 Facts: Exploring Space. Steve Parker, Miles Kelly Publishing, 2011.

Amazing Science Discoveries: Astronomy – The Story of Stars and Galaxies. Bryson Gore, Franklin Watts, 2009.

Machines Close-up: Space Vehicles. Daniel Gilpin, Wayland, 2012.

See Inside Space. Katie Daynes, Usborne Publishing, 2008.

Space: A Children's Encyclopedia. Dorling Kindersley, 2010.

Space Guides: Discovering the Universe. Peter Grego, QED Publishing, 2008.

Space Travel Guides: Space Exploration. Giles Sparrow, Franklin Watts, 2013.

Websites

To find out about all the current missions in which NASA are involved, go to:
http://solarsystem.nasa.gov/missions/profile.cfm?InFlight=1

For facts and information about the planets in our solar system, go to NASA's website at:
http://solarsystem.nasa.gov/planets/profile.cfm?Object=SolarSys

Find out about the Universe at the European Space Agency's website for children:
www.esa.int/esaKIDSen/OurUniverse.html

This section of the European Space Agency's website includes information about the International Space Station with links to astronauts and the search for life on other planets:
www.esa.int/esaKIDSen/SpaceStations.html

See for yourself what it is like to live and work on the International Space Station. In these video clips an astronaut takes you on an exciting tour of the Station:
www.nasa.gov/mission_pages/station/main/suni_iss_tour.html

INDEX